The Solar System

The Solar System 2
Stars 4
Day and Night 6
The Moon. 8
Seasons 10

Harcourt
SCHOOL PUBLISHERS

Orlando Austin New York San Diego Toronto London

Visit *The Learning Site!*
www.harcourtschool.com

The Solar System

The sun is the center of the solar system.
Nine planets move around the sun.
Earth is one of the planets.

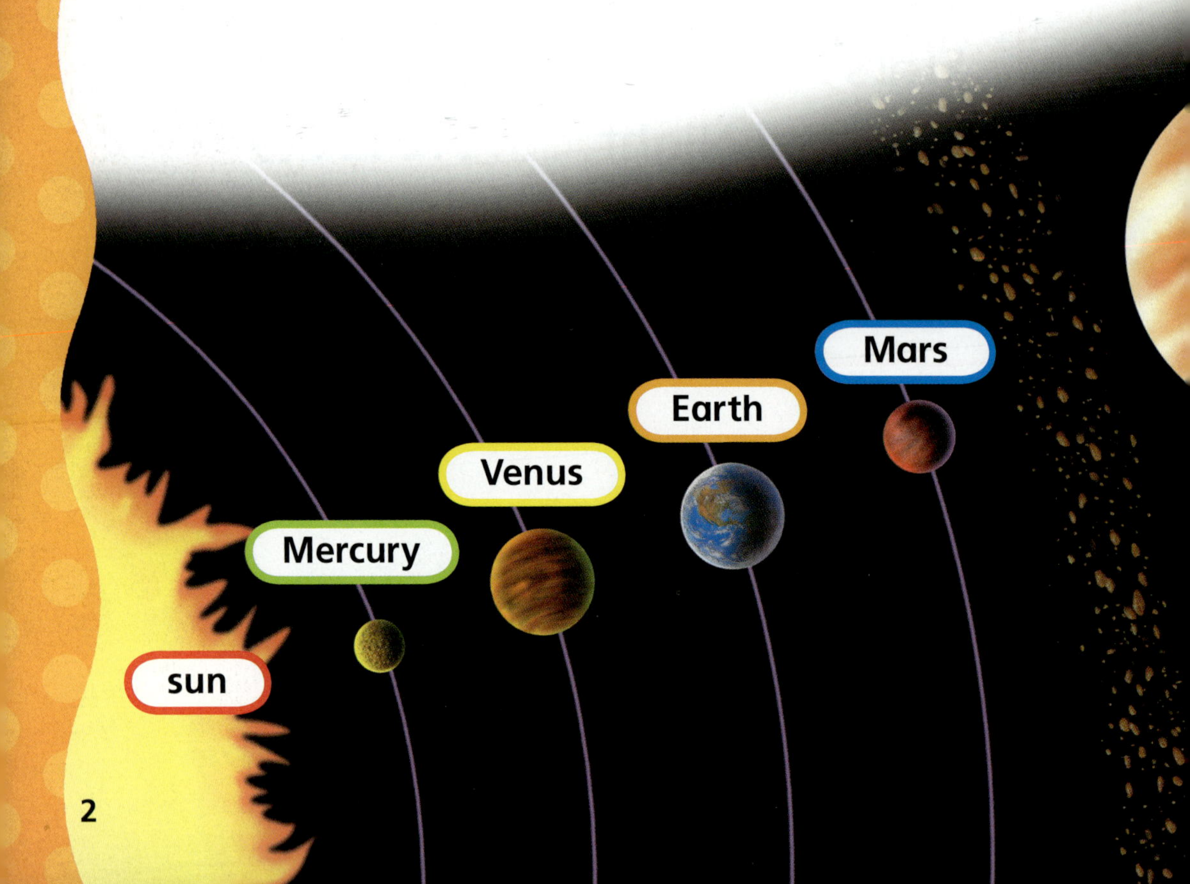

Planets are made of rock or gas.
Some planets have moons. Some do not.
Some are close to the sun. Some are not.
Each planet moves in its own orbit.

Stars

The sun is a star. It is made of hot gases. The hot gases give off light and heat. The sun is the closest star to Earth. We see other stars only at night.

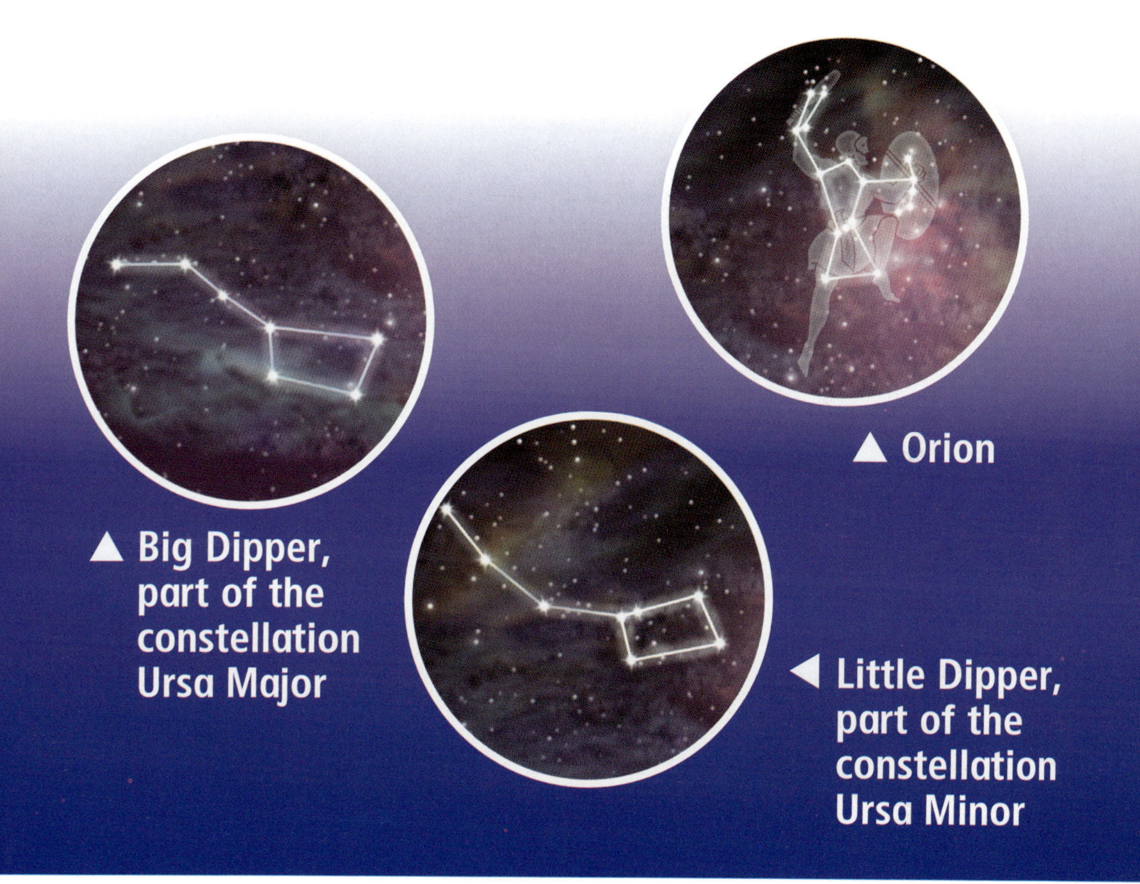

▲ Orion

▲ Big Dipper, part of the constellation Ursa Major

◀ Little Dipper, part of the constellation Ursa Minor

A group of stars may form a constellation.
A constellation is a pattern of stars.

Day and Night

The sun seems to move across the sky.
But the sun does not move. Earth moves.
Earth rotates, or spins like a top.
It takes about 24 hours to make one turn.

At times, our part of Earth faces the sun.
That is when we have day.
Then, our part faces away from the sun.
That is when we have night.

The Moon

The moon is a ball of rock.
It moves in an orbit around Earth.
One full orbit takes about a month.

The moon reflects light from the sun.
The part of the moon we see changes.
That is why its shape seems to change.

Seasons

Earth moves in an orbit around the sun. One full orbit takes about 365 days, a year. As Earth orbits, its tilt stays the same. That is why we have seasons.

At times, our part of Earth tilts toward the sun.
That is when we have summer.
Then, our part tilts away from the sun.
That is when we have winter.

Vocabulary

constellation, p. 5
moon, p. 8
orbit, p. 3
planet, pp. 2–3
rotate, p. 6
season, p. 10
solar system, p. 2
star, p. 4